In the Pursuit of Excellence:

A Concise Guide For Creating Unlimited Possibility in YOUR Life, Business and/or Organization!

by Robert Frutos

Text by Robert Frutos

ISBN-13: 978-1496015433

ePub ISBN-10: 1496015436

Also by Robert Frutos;

With Beauty All Around Me: Inspirations to Touch the Heart, Heal, and Uplift the Spirit, Walking in Beauty: Inspirational Seed Thoughts for Creating YOUR Best Life Possible! Photographing Nature in Hawaii: Capturing the Beauty & Spirit of the Islands, Hawaii Inspiration Aflame: A Passion for the Magnificence, Light on Hawaii: Capturing the Dynamic Islandscape A Photographers Approach, Clarity, Inspiration & Optimum Potential: A Concise Guide for Creating Infinite Possibility in YOUR life!

www.robertfrutos.com

www.lightofalohagreetings.com

www.heartofnature.net

www.hawaiiphototours.org

www.hawaiisacredsitestours.com

rfphoto@jps.net

808 345 – 7179

Cover Image by Robert Frutos

Dedication

To the pioneers, the visionaries, and the dreamers, who realize that *the seed to create the foundation for success and prosperity, not only in our businesses but in our daily lives – is to be found in the human imagination, in the human spirit, and our faith in the future!*

This handbook if used everyday, could radically transform, profoundly shape and dynamically create your ideal life, business, or organization!

Preface

This book was created by request.
A number of individuals from businesses and
organizations approached me after
reading: **Clarity, Inspiration, & Optimum
Potential: A Concise Guide for Creating Infinite
Possibility in YOUR Life!** and asked me to write
one that specifically applied to creating and/or
maintaining a successful and dynamic business
and/or organization.

**In the Pursuit of Excellence:
A Concise Guide for Creating Unlimited
Possibility in YOUR Life, Business and/or
Organization!**
is the result. It contains many of the techniques
and practices that are in the first book - it has to -
all of the same principles and course of actions
apply - but this book IS specifically applicable to
companies and organizations towards growing and
fostering a successful business/service based on
the dynamics of optimum potential that lead to
peak performance, increased productivity and
unlimited profitability.

So, if you are interested in creating infinite
potential in your own life - the top mentioned book
will serve you well.
**If you have a business or organization you are
inspiring to build, grow, thrive, and prosper -
then this is the book for you.**

Table of Context

Introduction

**"Excellence is going the extra mile
where failure refuses to go!"**

Each of us is unique and each of us is given an
extraordinary gift in life.

An opportunity to live our highest inspirations,
and seed, grow, and create our deepest dreams.

But why *excellence* as a means toward living the
life of our dreams?

Because the level of energy required for excellence
(in other words, the consciousness of excellence)
can and will propel us forward into an optimum
and unlimited flow of energy potential.

When we are in the flow of optimum potential,
we *can* begin to generate, draw, and create a
pathway towards a life of fulfillment, success,
happiness, and abundance.

So what is optimum potential, exactly?

**Optimum potential in one's life, comes with
aligning *one's highest inspirations*,
imagination, creativity and passion -**

**into an endless flow of energy that manifests
into our deepest dreams and overflows into our
everyday reality.**

And what is excellence, precisely?

True excellence begins *within* each individual, and evolves into an inspired inner attitude, such as: *I will give and share my gifts in life - in the very best way possible.*

Excellence may be the result of a group endeavor, but in each case, it starts with, and requires an individuals firm commitment regarding energy, focus, and awareness...

quickly evolving into qualities of: clear value, proficiency, brilliance, expertise and mastery.

Through the keen focus of excellence and optimum potential we begin the process to draw into our life the dynamic conditions, people, and circumstances, that help manifest the very steps that lead us towards the fulfillment of our goals, and our highest happiness.

In many positions through the years as – educator, counselor, business owner, healer, minister, and friend, I have had the opportunity (and great blessing) to hear and learn of many peoples' inspirations, dreams, passions, as well as their challenges, and difficulties. Along with the deep desire to live a more meaningful life - one of true aliveness, meaning & fulfillment.

At the same time, whenever I inquire:
"Why aren't you living your inspirations? What is keeping you from following your heart, and living your dreams?"

I get a multitude of answers, underlying the same response - all saying that for some reason or another, "it simply cannot be done."

The most common answers are:
"The timing is just not right yet" or,
"He, she, they, or it, are blocking or preventing me from moving forward, and doing what *I really want to do.*"

From this experience, I have discovered that many people have **unnecessarily** convinced themselves that whatever it is in life they ***really*** want remains... *just beyond their reach.*

And yet, there are **universal principles** and **universal laws**, that once understood and utilized, reveal quite the opposite to be true.

That in fact, we ***can*** create and manifest the life of our highest inspirations and deepest dreams. We **CAN** begin to shift our life view into a dynamic forward moving direction.

With the awareness of the nature of these laws and principles and the practice of these techniques that are available to anyone:
We can initiate real change into *our* life.

But where to start?

If you are sincerely seeking a pathway to excellence, success, and true happiness -

"In the Pursuit of Excellence
The Energetics of Optimum Potential"

offers dynamic, powerful, time - tested tools, and the wisdom, and insights to achieve these goals.

To begin: All you have to do is include one marvelous word in your life. A simple word we are all familiar with: the "Y" word, the **"Yes!"** word. All we have to do is begin to say "**Yes to Life!**"

For **yes** is not just a word, it is *a state of mind and heart that we bring to life. Say* **yes** *to life and life will say* **yes** *to you. Saying* **Yes** *to life opens the gate to receiving what your heart and soul really want!*

As my wonderful friend, Derek Van Atta shares in his inspiring book: **Your Abundance Now: "Yes, is one of the most powerful words** we ever use. *The full - hearted feeling of* **"Yes"** *is full of freedom.*

Miracles occur from the consciousness of **Yes!** *You can move mountains with a no-holds-bar* **Yes!** *When you feel* **" Yes "** *in every cell in your body, you are in touch with the power of* **All** *Life!"*

When you say **"Yes to Life"** *you embrace life itself rather than brace up against it. Again, saying* **"yes to life"** *puts you in touch with the* **power** *of* **ALL** *life and aligns you with the awesome awareness* **that ALL things are possible!**

All you have to do is take the first step - and a process begins that generates the flow of energy towards creating, manifesting, and living the life of your highest inspirations.

The book you now hold in your hands will help you achieve these goals and is based on **time - proven** methods, insights, and experiences, which create the foundation for success and fulfillment - both essential components of a life well - lived.

This book is filled with inspiration and in - the - field, tried and true techniques, for creating and manifesting a sure - fire pathway toward living *your* highest inspirations!

Enjoy!

And may you wholeheartedly begin living the life you were meant to live: *a life of boundless inspiration, a life of wondrous joy, the life of your deepest dreams and your highest happiness!*

Robert "Govinda" Frutos

The real source of wealth and capital in this new era is not material things... it is the human mind, the human spirit, the human imagination, and our faith in the future.

~ Steve Forbes

"Follow your heart and intuition, they already know what you truly want to become.

Everything else is secondary."

~ Steve Jobs

1

Where Inspiration Lives!

*"At the height of inspiration
the universe is flung into a kaleidoscope
of new possibilities."*

True inspiration comes to us in quiet moments...
while the mind is calm and the heart is open.

True inspiration can come to us while walking
through a forest, sitting near a waterfall, or
watching the sunset.

True inspiration can come to us while relaxing
in our back yard.

True inspiration can come to us driving down the
highway, or while engaged in an uplifting activity -
such as listening to serene music, or enjoying
beautiful art.

When we engage in activities that: *ignite our sense
of inner joy, nurture our soul, relax and rejuvenate
our bodies, and refresh our minds,*
we find ourselves newly invigorated and inspired.

Through the portal of inspiration *our awareness is
lifted upwards* - into higher, and ever - increasing
levels of **"inner clarity"...inner clarity is** *the first
all - important step to creating a life
of inspired living and optimum possibility.*

__Inner clarity helps establish a blueprint__ - necessary to build the strong foundation that will enable you to create, develop, and shape, your highest happiness by allowing you clear vision.

There is a saying:
"If you don't know where you are heading, any road will get you there."

So the first real step *to create a life of inspired living and optimum possibility is to have a vision of what you truly want in life.* __Inner clarity__ helps crystalize your inspiration(s) and gives insight into the direction, and to the pathway that will lead you there.

__*Inner clarity is the inner compass that gives birth to a forward moving direction & crystal clear vision.*__

The most successful and effective way to leap directly into your new life direction, once inner clarity is achieved is through __*inspiration.*__ __Inspiration is born when the mind is calm and the heart is open.__

Inspiration often begins as a " whisper " in the mind, a "feeling" in the heart, or an unexpected flash of recognition. And regardless of when, where, or how inspiration unveils itself to you if you are sincere in your quest, you have only one true choice - to *inwardly listen* to its call.

As you sojourn forth... your quest will necessarily take you into the farthest reaches of your

creativity, and towards the farthest depths
of your imagination.

Traversing the unknown – the journey becomes an
exhilarating pathway into discovery and
exploration, inspiration and resourcefulness,
artistry and purposeful vision.

While the journey takes courage and can be at
times, a solitary experience, its efforts are
rewarded with the ever - increasing realization
that there are _NO_ limits and _ALL_ is possible.

*Living your highest inspirations - you will be
fulfilled in the life you have chosen and the promise
of the adventure it brings.*

For each of us is given an extraordinary gift. An
opportunity to live our highest inspirations: to
seed, grow, and create our deepest dreams.

From that pure place of *inner clarity*
& *inner knowing*, within ourselves, a light shines,
and grows stronger and brighter with each choice
we make - to stay true to our inner calling, to stay
true to our inner whispers.

We are given choices, moment by moment, hour
by hour, day by day. Make the choices that allow
your inner light to glow ever - more radiant.
Make the choices that that allow the doors to open
into YOUR highest happiness!

**"The future belongs to those
who believe in the beauty
of their dreams."**

~ Eleanor Roosevelt

2

There are No Obstacles, Only Opportunities

"What you are, has been created by the choices you have made thus far.

What you will become is determined by the choices you BEGIN to make NOW."

Our successes and failures in life, are determined *by the choices we make in each moment of our everyday life.*

Once you determine to change your direction towards having the best life possible, many new opportunities will come forth, including the opportunity of new challenges.

For change naturally means adjustments and modifications, As a result, friends may fall away, you may choose different career path, or even a new environment, one that suits and/or inspires the new you.

And be aware, your old world may decide to try and hold on to you. Your habits and patterns may be very strong and not want to easily give way to your new direction. When ever a big change comes into our life - these are often the times when we

17

are most vulnerable, and we need inner strength to overcome the influences that will attempt to block our new life direction.

"Life is an endlessly creative experience, and we are shaping ourselves at every moment by every decisions we make. "

~ Kent Nerburn

So listen not to others who would attempt to discourage you. Who would hold you back - keeping you from soaring upward into the skies beyond your wildest imaginings.

Heed not to circumstances that appear to block your aspirations, nor to conditions, that seemingly mirror the impossible, and call out to you – *it cannot be done!*

Listen foremost to the stirrings of your inner whispers, constantly calling to you, and reminding you of your highest inspirations, and deepest dreams.

Dare to be your true Self and offer to all your blessings of gratitude and keep moving forward, knowing that you are following the dream that beckons you onward... toward a life of success and joy and its ultimate prize - **real happiness**.

Though it be fraught with challenges and difficulties, its fulfillment - **your true happiness**, is its greatest bounty and reward.

Let others define their own limits in life and create
the confines of their own imaginings - if need be.
Let others be happy in the world that they have
chosen for themselves.

And while there will be moments when clarity,
intent and direction all come together in an easy
flow to manifest your deepest dreams
and highest happiness.

There will also be moments when we feel we have
become momentarily stuck and it appears our
path has become unclear and/or even blocked.

*"The secret of change is to focus
all of your energy,
not on fighting the old,
but building the new."*

~Socrates

To be sure, obstacles and difficulties will come our
way. They are part and parcel to the journey -even
more than that, they are an necessary ingredient.

*They breathe new life into our determination, shape
our fortitude, and help build our inner resolve.* They
are meant to test us, to make us strive onward.

*They compel us to stretch, and then stretch again,
just beyond our reach -* to achieve our intentions
and goals.

And for every challenge and/or difficulty that we work to overcome, *our intent becomes more determined, our inner light burns brighter, our will power increases exponentially, and our true vision becomes more radiantly clear.*

Obstacles and difficulties help define who we are, and what we are made of.

Be glad for them, for by overcoming them we are lifted to unequaled heights of new understanding, insight, and ever - increasing awareness.

Once the trials pass, we are free to soar on the wings of ever - more and greater inspiration, inner joy, and **complete** aliveness.

As we begin to align ourselves with inner clarity, imagination, and creativity, and turn our passion into a strong, clear direction, our focus and intention thus concentrated has a most powerful effect; that not only propels us forward, but ***through*** any influences that come between us and our inspired goals.

While we cannot control the world around us, we can control how we choose to respond to anything that effects ***our*** world.

Through our conscious choices, focused attention, and new intention, we begin to magnetize and create a ***new*** reality in our life, and the world around us.

By our choices, thus far, we have created our present lives.

By our choices, thus far, we have determined what we will continue to attract into our lives - unless and until, we consciously change our choices.

Most importantly, by the choices we make from this moment forth, we determine what entirely new set of dynamic events, circumstances, and people we will **NOW** begin to attract into our lives that will help create and support our new life direction.

The most successful person directs and holds their attention and intent by conscious choice.

In this way we can begin to change our lives into an inspirational flow, that grows and blooms, into and towards, our highest happiness.

*"There are no obstacles,
only opportunities."*

~ Paramhansa Yogananda

3
Be a Magnet of Happiness!

"There is no way to Happiness, Happiness is the way."

~ Buddha

True happiness begins simply by determining to be happy - regardless of circumstances, persons, or events.

Just for a moment, think of a time in your life - when you were **really happy!** Close your eyes and relive that experience for a few moments, or a few minutes.

Now close your eyes, again. Think of a place you like to visit, your favorite place... whether it be the ocean, a forest, or a hike in the solitude of the desert.

Wherever it be, let it be a place that nourishes you, and refreshes you. Clearly see yourself there. Allow yourself to relive the experiences that makes it special for you.

For example, let's say your favorite place is the ocean. See yourself, sitting by the shore or laying on the beach. Mentally observe that its a magnificently beautiful day with big billowing white clouds. You gently let the lapping waves lull you into a *deep, deep, deeper* relaxation.
You feel in harmony and at peace.

23

The warm sun surrounds you. You feel its warmth seeping into the depths of your being, and it fills you with a deeper relaxation. A gentle wind is blowing and there is soft laughter in the distant.

You may continue to imagine the experience, the location, the setting, and the sensations for as long as you like, but the real question here is:

HOW DOES IT MAKE YOU FEEL?

Happy, of course, but what's the over-all feeling? **Isn't it an *UP* feeling? Isn't it an *UP* energy? When you're happy (inspired) your energy is up!**

When you have that *up* feeling there is a sense of excitement, anticipation, and expectation.

You feel within, regardless of what may be presenting itself in that moment, that everything is not only going to work out in your favor - **it's going to work out perfectly, and in the best way possible!**

This *up* feeling, this *up* energy - doesn't it feel as if it permeates your every atom? Every fiber of your being feels completely alive - dynamic and magnetic, and you are filled with unbounded enthusiasm and spontaneous joy!

This *up* energy, this *up* feeling that you have inside yourself - *IS THE MAGNET.*

The magnet that starts to draw to you everything you need... **TO MAKE YOUR DREAM BECOME A LIVING REALITY.**

When you're **up**, you have all your energy focused in a clear, positive, and single - minded direction, *there is nearly nothing that can stop you from moving forward into your fullest optimum potential and towards the achievement of your inspired goals.*

If we focus dynamically and wholeheartedly on the happy/inspired **UP** energy - **we create the magnet *within* ourselves** that takes us toward our intended goal, and " magnetically " draws to us whatever we need, as we take our very next step... each step of the way.

If we focus on our doubts - the cant's, and wont's - of our life, we block our own, and the universal flow of energy - that is trying to cooperate in the creation of our infinite possibilities, and the fulfillment of our highest inspirations.

"Our intention creates our reality."

~ Wayne Dyer

*"If you think you can do a thing,
or think you can't do a thing,
you're right."*

~ Henry Ford

4

The True Power
of "Positive Thinking" Revealed!

*"O God, help me to believe
the truth about myself,
no matter how beautiful it is."*

You most likely have heard of "the power of
positive thinking." Positive thinking can lead you
quickly forward, and help jump start your efforts
on the road to success and joy.

Positive thinking is simply about looking at things
from a positive point of view. Positive thinking
means approaching life's challenges
with a positive outlook:

trying to see the best in other people, viewing
yourself and your abilities in a positive light,
and it includes making the most of potentially
bad situations.

The story below illustrates the "power"
of positive thinking:

Jerry was the kind of guy you love to hate.
He was always in a good mood and always had
something positive to say. When someone would
ask him how he was doing, he would reply,

"If I were any better, I would be twins!"

He was a unique manager because he had several waiters who had followed him around from restaurant to restaurant. The reason the waiters followed Jerry was because of his attitude.

He was a natural motivator. If an employee was having a bad day, Jerry was there telling the employee how to look on the positive side of the situation.

Seeing this style really made me curious, so one day I went up to Jerry and asked him, "I don't get it! You can't be a positive person all of the time. How do you do it?"

Jerry replied, "Each morning I wake up and say to myself, Jerry, you have two choices today. You can choose to be in a good mood or you can choose to be in a bad mood.' I choose to be in a good mood.

Each time something bad happens, I can choose to be a victim or I can choose to learn from it. I choose to learn from it. Every time someone comes to me complaining, I can choose to accept their complaining or I can point out the positive side of life. I choose the positive side of life."

"Yeah, right, it's not that easy," I protested.
"Yes it is," Jerry said. "Life is all about choices. When you cut away all the junk, every situation is a choice. You choose how you react to situations. You choose how people will affect your mood. You choose to be in a good mood or bad mood.

The bottom line: It's your choice how you live life."

I reflected on what Jerry said. Soon thereafter, I left the restaurant industry to start my own business. We lost touch, but often thought about him when I made a choice about life instead of reacting to it.

Several years later, I heard that Jerry did something you are never supposed to do in a restaurant business: he left the back door open one morning and was held up at gunpoint by three armed robbers.

While trying to open the safe, his hand, shaking from nervousness, slipped off the combination. The robbers panicked and shot him.

Luckily, Jerry was found relatively quickly and rushed to the local trauma center. After 18 hours of surgery and weeks of intensive care, Jerry was released from the hospital with fragments of the bullets still in his body.

I saw Jerry about six months after the accident. When I asked him how he was, he replied, "If I were any better, I'd be twins. Wanna see my scars?"

I declined to see his wounds, but did ask him what had gone through his mind as the robbery took place. "The first thing that went through my mind was that I should have locked the back door," Jerry replied.

"Then, as I lay on the floor, I remembered that I had two choices: I could choose to live, or I could choose to die. I chose to live."

"Weren't you scared? Did you lose consciousness?" I asked. Jerry continued, "The paramedics were great. They kept telling me I was going to be fine. But when they wheeled me into the emergency room and I saw the expressions on the faces of the doctors and nurses, I got really scared.

In their eyes, I read, 'He's a dead man.' I knew I needed to take action. "What did you do?" I asked. "Well, there was a big, burly nurse shouting questions at me," said Jerry.

"She asked if I was allergic to any-thing. 'Yes,' I replied. The doctors and nurses stopped working as they waited for my reply...

I took a deep breath and yelled, 'Bullets!' Over their laughter, I told them, 'I am choosing to live. Operate on me as if I am alive, not dead."

Jerry lived thanks to the skill of his doctors, but also because of his amazing attitude. I learned from him that every day we have the choice to live fully.

The above story reveals how strongly potent our thoughts really are!

Everyday, every hour, every moment we are given the opportunity, the choices, and the kind of actions - that will keep us anchored to our present reality or give us the wings to soar into our newly inspired vision of reality.

Again, while we cannot control the world around us, we can control how we choose to respond to anything that effects **our** world. Through our conscious choices, focused attention, and intention, we begin to magnetize and create a **new** reality in our life, and the world around us.

Positive thinking and being positive is a prime ingredient in success of any kind. However, the real secret behind being successful with positive thinking is *FEELING!*
FEELING it - as well as thinking it.

In order to be a **true magnet** (in other words, to become truly magnetic) you not only have to be thinking positively to manifest your new reality, but most importantly,
You need to *FEEL* it as well...
as though it is already happening, **Now!**
As though it is **a living, thriving reality, Now!**

Feeling and thought combined **create the magnet, the stronger the feeling - the stronger the thought - the stronger the magnet(ism).**

When you have the feeling of unbound enthusiasm combined with spontaneous joy – a total and complete sense of uplifted feeling - *that creates and is,* **our inner magnet.**

For example, projecting *a strong thought and clear*

feeling that "everything will work out for the best," as did the chief minister - regardless of outward circumstances - energetically draws the reality that *will* allow **everything to work out in best possibly way.**

~ O ~

There is a story of a bus driver
that was taking a group of people
from one town to the next.

On the way, the bus driver decided
to give a short break to everyone,
a chance to stretch out and get
some fresh air, and he pulled off
to the side of the road.

After several minutes when they
all got on the bus to go again
the bus driver closed the door,
started the engine, and stepped
on the accelerator.

The bus did not move.

He tried again, and still the bus
did not move. He got off and looked
around the bus, only to find that he
had pulled off the road a little too far.

On one side of the bus the rear wheels
had been softly spinning in the sand.

He thought for a moment and then

realized with just a little push,
he could get the bus out of the
sandy area, back on the road,
and onward they could go.

So he climbed back into the bus
and asked everyone to get off the bus
and help push - just a little, so they could
get out of the sand, and back on the road
to continue their journey.

Everyone got off the bus and began
to push. ***The bus did not move,
the bus would not budge***.

The bus driver yelled out, "push" again,
"this time harder" and everybody pushed
and still the bus did not move.

So the bus driver said,
"wait just a darn minute, here."

And he walked across to the other side
of the road to gain perspective. To see
if there was anything that was keeping
the bus from being allowed to be
pushed forward.

In doing so, as he looked back across
the road - he realized that half the people
were pushing on the front of the bus,
and the other half were pushing
on the back of the bus.

He then asked everyone to move

to the back end of the bus and push
forward, and when they did so -
the bus easily moved forward
out of the sand, back onto the road,
and away they all merrily went.

~ O ~

And isn't this how most people live their lives?

Half the time pushing their minds, thoughts, and
hearts in one direction, the other half, pushing
them in the opposite direction.

It doesn't take much to see why things don't move
forward with a steady ease and flow.

If we are constantly pushing our energies in
opposite directions or into one another how can
we ever move forward?

**But when our energy is *UP*, and clear,
and energetic** (and therefore magnetic) and
we are really **FEELING positive and uplifted -
*what in the world can stop us?***

***"You never change things
by fighting the existing reality.
To change something, build a new model
that makes the existing model obsolete."***

~ Buckminster Fuller

5

With Our Thoughts
We Make the World!

*"As a single footstep will not make a path
on the earth, so a single thought will not
make a pathway in the mind.*

*To make a deep physical path, we walk
again and again.*

*To make a deep mental path, we must
think over and over the kind of thoughts
we wish to dominate our lives."*

~ Henry David Thoreau

Every thought you think, every word you say,
every feeling you experience, automatically
generates its own individual & unique energy.

If you think and send out thoughts of success and
kindness, then you will draw into your life a world
oriented towards success & kindness.

If you think and send out thoughts of failure and
fear, then you will draw into your life a world
oriented towards failure and fear.

*This is one of the laws of the Universe:
you can only draw the same amount,*

and kind of energy that you originally
send out into the world.

It is thought first - then action that begins the process to generate the manifestation of a new reality. Again, as mentioned above, if your **strong focus** is on success and kindness, then that is what you will draw repeatedly to yourself in life.

If, on the other hand, your focus is on what is ***not*** working in your life, often mixed with thoughts and feelings of anger, bitterness, or resentment (negative emotions are all energy blocks in themselves) then you will repeatedly draw ***those*** kind of experiences into your life.

Thus, We Create Our Own Reality
by the Power of Our Thought(s).

Our thoughts are like seeds, and they can only grow according to their own nature - otherwise **it would be like planting tomato seeds and expecting carrots to come up.**

So, choose your thoughts wisely, choose to be positive, ***regardless*** of what conditions may come, in doing so we draw to ourselves the right people, and the right set of circumstances, that allow us to break through our own (and others) imposed limitations.

This sanctions us to move forward - into our optimum potential - toward achievement, fulfillment, and success. Like being happy - being positive requires no conditions, events, or circumstances to set it into motion.

Merely by determining to be happy - we draw happiness in our lives. Merely by choosing to be positive - we draw positive experiences into our lives.

You are NOW fully aware of why and how our thoughts and feelings are so significance and how they **literally create and shape our life.**

With the awareness of how our thoughts and feelings create our reality - you are given a new opportunity to create (recreate) the best life possible *by focusing on what you really want in life and making* the best possible choices for achieving these goals.

Congratulations - by being aware and conscious of how *YOU* create your world - beginning with your thoughts and feelings, you can acknowledge the world you have created for yourself, thus far.

Now begin to CHANGE your life - beginning with your thoughts - into the world you aspire to!

"We are what we think.
All that we are arises with our thoughts.
With our thoughts we make the world."

~ Buddha

6

Creating the Life You Aspire To!

"It is your thoughts and acts of the moment - that create your future."

It has been scientifically proven that we have an average of 60,000 thoughts per day. If you are an above average thinker then you have approximately 75,000 thoughts a day. And if you are
very deep thinker, more advanced like Einstein, then you may have up to 90,000 thoughts per day.

Even at 60,000 thoughts per day... that is equal to 2500 thoughts per hour, or 41.6 thoughts per minute. Of the 60,000 thoughts we have each day, 98% of the thoughts are the same thoughts we had the day before (this too has been scientifically proven).

Of the 98% of the thoughts we had yesterday that we are having again today - an average of 50% are negative thoughts.

Moreover, thoughts really *are* powerful, as thoughts *are* energy. The stronger they are - the more focused and magnetic they become. They act as magnets that draw in our lives the people, circumstances and events, that become our daily life.

How do you spend time? - and where do spend time with your thoughts each day?
How many are positive and how many are negative? Do you focus on lack or do you focus on abundance? Where you direct the quality of your thoughts, whether positive or negative, *brings you the direct experience of those same kind of thought seeds.*

Again, with our thoughts we make the world and the experiences of our reality everyday.

Now lets focus on how to change and shift our thoughts to bring in the reality and lifestyle that we aspire to create...

on the following pages are a number of time - proven techniques. They will give you the insights and tools not only to get you going in the right direction, but help you create a world of inspired living and peak optimum potential.

These techniques may not be new to you. Perhaps you are already practicing and applying some of them in your daily life – if they are effective and helpful in moving you forward in your new life direction - excellent!

You may, however, find techniques included here that you are not presently applying, altogether new to you, and perhaps more productive.

Adding these specific valuable techniques to your daily activities will prove both unerringly beneficial and powerfully effective and begin to draw success

& abundance into YOUR life. They include *affirmations, visualizations, and meditations.*

These techniques and methods are all ways to get your energy, thoughts, and vision, into a clear focus and dynamically move them forward in a united direction.

Building a foundation of the techniques is exceptionally helpful in creating an understanding of one of the most important aspects of living an inspired life.

By practicing the techniques, you will learn how to "listen inwardly." This is also known as "intuitive awareness."

Through "intuitive awareness" we can access the deeper pools of Universal wisdom. The wisdom that allows us to inwardly know best - when to do what, how, and when, to achieve the best possible results.

The Hawaiian word for this is **"Kina ola:"** **"Doing the right thing, the right way, at the right time, in the right place, to the right person, for the right reason, with the right feeling... the first time."**

Again, it all begins with our thoughts. So let's start by taking the first step - let's begin filling our established, perhaps stubborn and routine, present thought patterns - ***with newly***

40

inspired and conscious choice thought patterns (so as to replace the thoughts that keep us in the same old patterns of living.)

Creating **New** thoughts **will begin** to manifest our new reality - inner clarity, inspired living and ever - increasing joy, the thought seeds that will grow into the fulfillment of our deepest dreams!

"Only as high as I reach can I grow,
only as far as I seek can I go,
only as deep as I look can I see,
only as much as I dream can I be."

~ Karen Ravn

Within each moment lies the infinite
potential for you to be
what your deepest Self aspires to be.

7

Affirmations – Seeds for Manifesting Change Now!

**" Excellence is a process,
a quality of mind and a way of being,
an outgoing affirmation of life. "**

*AN AFFIRMATION IS A PROJECTED
THOUGHT:* it is a statement of truth that can
become absorbed and activated into our lives with
profound and immediate results.

Using affirmations as a tool, we can effectively
draw into our lives the attributes, and qualities –
we are dynamically and powerfully affirming.

If we desire success or abundance, for example,
we simply begin to affirm these qualities.

**By the focused projection of our thought,
an energy is set into motion that creates
the magnetism that begins to draw that
reality to us, and makes that reality
a part of our everyday life.**

When our **intent** and **focus** are **strong** enough,
we automatically draw experiences of success and
abundance into our lives. As well as the people,
places, and environments, that will bring us
success and abundance.

It is a universal law, that what we focus our attention on, is what we draw into our life. The Hawaiian way of saying this is: *"Energy Flows where Attention Goes."* We have all had experiences of this in our life.

Lets take a likely common experience as an example... say its a nice warm summer day, and your longing for something cool and refreshing.

You see somebody with an ice cream cone, and the thought occurs to you that you would *really* like to have an ice cream cone. You don't give it much more thought, but it keeps appearing and reappearing in the back of your mind.

And soon you begin to think more and more, of just how delightful and refreshing it would be to have a nice refreshing ice cream cone.

As the thought begins to gather momentum, you think of the many wonderful times you've had an ice cream cone. You think about the many different kinds of ice cream cones you had... you give thought to your most favorite ice cream cone. Pretty soon, ice cream cones are not only the upper most, but the strongest thought in your mind, and you absolutely have to have an ice cream cone.

Your thoughts and your intention have become so strong - that all you can do is turn your full attention towards getting a nice, refreshing, and thirst quenching ice cream cone.

And so, you WILL get an ice cream cone.

For the ice cream cone, we can substitute a candy bar, a new pair of running shoes, a blouse, a car, a house, etc. - the list is endless, but the process is the same... the thought arises, then becomes stronger.

Then becomes stronger still. Then becomes upper most in your mind, mixed with strong intention. And finally our will - jumps in the process to procure the desired delicacy or item, until at last, we have it not only within reach, but in our hands (don't forget the napkins).

Now taking this process into the realm of affirmation, it is the same course of action - first the thought (affirmation) arises, Then becomes stronger, then becomes stronger still.

Then becomes upper most in your mind, mixed with strong intention. And finally your full attention and will – jump into absorb and procure the desired quality and/or outcome of the specific affirmation.

Until at last, we have it not only within reach, but it becomes a part of our everyday reality.

Ultimately positive thoughts are the only thoughts - that we want to be focusing our minds and attention on, and that fully contribute to our creating the life of our dreams. As you will observe, all of the below listed affirmations *are* fully **positive.**

The specific kind of affirmation(s) you will choose to give your attention to, is determined by the qualities or attributes you want to create in your life *in this moment.* Affirmations can be short, simple, empowering statements.

For example:

For drawing success and abundance:

" Life fills me with success and abundance "

To be ready and open
for any possibility and/or any circumstance:

**" I'm Awake and Ready,
I'm Awake and Ready "**

For positiveness and fortitude:

" I am positive, energetic, enthusiastic, "

or, as a company/ business/organization:

**" With focused and united purpose
our efforts bring forth
success and abundance. "**

For drawing friendship
and laughter into your work environment:

**" I am/we are are surrounded by
friends and laughter. "**

For inner and outer harmony in your place
of business:

**" I am/we are one
with the harmony of all life. "**
Affirmations can also be longer -
according to what you are focusing on
and calling into your life
in that moment.

Below are a number of examples
of affirmations for manifesting different qualities
into your life.

For Success:

*I leave behind me both my failures
and my accomplishments.
What I do today will create
a new and better future,
filled with inner joy.*

Will Power:

*My will is that which is right to do.
Part, all you mountains
that stand in my way!
Nothing can stop my progress!*

Inspiration:

*I hold my thoughts up
to the calmness within;*

in calmness
I receive inspiration.

Calmness:

Though the winds of difficulties
howl around me,
I stand forever calmly
at the center of life's storms.

The above affirmations are from "**Affirmations for Self-Healing**," by J. Donald Walters, published by Crystal Clarity Publishing. Used with kind permission from the author.

The above affirmations are powerful and effective. Along with these, there are many different types of affirmations, and many excellent affirmations books.

To foray into the many possibilities, simply google "affirmations" or "affirmation books" and see the list of resources available,

or, another option - is to create your own affirmations, according to the specific aspirations of your personal goals (see short simple affirmations listed above for creative ideas).

The idea is to choose one or two affirmations that resonate deeply within you, and what you want to presently create and draw into
in your life.

Here is an affirmation example
specifically for a business/organization:

**" We are going to be the best
because we deserve to work at the best
(name of company or organization optional)
and our efforts deserve to be recognized
as the most admired effort
in the most admired company. "**

The power and effectiveness of affirmations is
shared by J Donald Walters:

*"By strongly and deliberately
affirming positive qualities,
with FULL awareness
and with DEEP concentration,
one can undo,
even in a few minutes
the negative effects of a lifetime."*

"Make of your life an affirmation,
defined by your ideals,
not the negation of others.

Dare to the level of your capabilities,
then go beyond to a higher level."

~ Alexander Haig

8

Affirmations –
the Most Effective Results

*" Everything is energy
and that's all there is to it.
Match the frequency of the reality
you want and you cannot help
but get that reality. It can be no other way.
This is not philosophy. This is physics.*

(physics = the branch of science concerned with
the nature and properties of matter and energy.)

~ Albert Einstein

1

The Most Effective Way

The most effective way to practice affirmations is
to focus on your chosen affirmation(s) with **deep
concentration.**

First, vigorously and assertively – repeat
the affirmation verbally several times.

Then again, still vigorously but not as assertively -
repeat the affirmation several times.

Now repeat in a quiet whisper several times,

then, with strong intent and deep feeling, repeat mentally (silently) several times.

2

The Best Time

The best time to affirm affirmations is just before going to sleep and first thing upon awaking in the morning. These times are the most potent and therefore will have the most powerful effect.

Why?

Because as we ready ourselves to give into sleep, our mind begins to shift from conscious awareness to subconscious awareness.

The subconscious mind is where most of our self - created blocks: such as doubt - the cant's and wont's - in our lives hide and thrive, just beneath the surface of our conscious awareness.

As we affirm and repeat our affirmations at these times of day, they deeply affect our subconscious mind. The energy and momentum of our focused affirmation continue " working " in the sub- conscious mind throughout the night.

Again, repeating the affirmation(s) immediately upon awakening while still in the semi - state of subconsciousness strongly affects the sub - conscious mind, as well as planting the seed thoughts into the conscious mind for the day.

Practicing affirmations at these times of day goes most directly into our subconscious mind and begins to dismantle the cant's, wont's, and do not's, that attempt to continue living there.

The effectiveness of this practice can be simply tested by repeating and affirming how tired or exhausted you are feeling - as you lay in bed to fall asleep. Guaranteed, you will wake up feeling exhausted, regardless of how many hours you actually sleep.

On the other hand, if you mentally affirm as you drift off into deep slumber this affirmation:

"I am positive, energetic, enthusiastic"
"I am positive, energetic, enthusiastic"

you will then arise ready to greet the new day with enthusiasm and energy!

Why not then, repeat the specific affirmations with the focus and energy that you want to draw and absorb into your life. Repeating them, as directed above, allows them to both become firmly rooted and flourish within the many levels of our awareness - our sub-conscious, conscious & superconscious awareness (intuitive awareness).

Once you begin to practice in the above manner – the affirmations will become second nature. They can then be repeated anytime, anywhere, whether walking, driving, or quietly sitting, verbally or silently, all the while repeating with firm intention and deep feeling.

This simple, yet powerful technique, and the potent impetus it creates allows you to set into motion the energy towards creating the world you want to manifest: **Now! – the world of your optimum energy potential, abundance, and success.**

9

Creative Visualization: Turning Your Dreams into Reality!

" You can't do it unless you imagine it. "

~ George Lucas

VISUALIZATION IS THE ART OF PROJECTING OUR VISION!

Each time we focus and mentally imagine what we want our new life to look like - we unite our creativity and imagination - to " see " a vision of that/our new reality,

As with the affirmations - visualization creates an energy that sets into motion the magnetism that begins to draw our new reality.

Affirmation uses the power and energetics of positive thought. Visualization by passes the verbalizing function of the brain, and in doing so brings into play the creative art of imagination.

You can then begin to focus and achieve whatever you choose, *for there are few things more powerful than effective visualization followed by action.*

We unknowingly have been practicing this technique all our lives. Only we have been doing so without conscious intention.

More often than not we have been unwittingly and unconsciously visualizing, and focusing on our problems rather than our inspirations; visualizing and focusing on our frustrations and limitations, rather than our desired goals and what really inspires us and fuels our passion.

By utilizing creative visualization, *we use our imagination to create new and positive mental images, that supersede our current mental images, and trigger the spirit of success.*

The most effective visualization is done by focusing our imagination into a mental image, or " picture " of what you want to manifest in your life.

Then allowing yourself to experience **the actual feeling - of what that experience would be like, as if you were fully and completely living in the manifestation of its reality, NOW, as if its already in place, and the great joy it brings!**

You do not have to focus on the exact details of what you want, **but most importantly focus on the feeling -** the **UP feeling**, the **UP energy,** how it would it *feel -* if it *IS* in reality, **already in place? Already a living, thriving reality?**

For example, take the need for a car:

You would clearly and vividly focus
on the joy of having and being in the car
(remember that UP feeling)?

See yourself driving the car,
allowing yourself to be
completely absorbed in the
experience of driving the car.

Perhaps even seeing yourself
driving down the road
with the windows down
on a beautiful spring morning;
smelling all the new smells
of spring: flowers, trees in bloom
& newly mowed lawns;

listening to music that uplifts you
and enhances the total experience
adding to the beauty of the day,
as if in harmony with the
symphony of all life.

Certainly enjoy the comfort
of the seats, the ease of steering,
revel in the smooth quiet ride,
the delight of the scenery around you.

You do not even have to necessarily
focus on the specific type of car you want,
or even the color. You most importantly need
to focus and visualize on the experience
of either having, or driving,
or being in the car -

AND Again,
allowing yourself to fully **FEEL** as though **it is
already in place, a living, thriving, reality -
Now!**

*"Imagination is more important
than knowledge!
Logic will get you from A to B.
Imagination will take you everywhere."*

~ Albert Einstein

The first step towards accomplishing successful
and creative visualization **is to learn to relax
deeply.** So lets go ahead and give it a try!

**Exercise 1:
Visualization**

Here are instructions for a simple,
yet powerful visualization:

*find a place to sit quietly
and comfortably,
close your eyes and
take a few deep breathes.*

*Continuing with eyes closed,
put your mental gaze gently upward
at the point between the eyebrows.*

*Inhale, counting mentally from 1 - 8
hold the breathe, counting mentally from 1 - 8*

and exhale as you count mentally 1 - 8.

Do this cycle of inhaling, holding,
and releasing the breath 3 - 4 times.
Then mentally observe the natural flow
of your breath.

You may become aware of the flow
of your breath through the mental
observation of the rise and fall of your
belly as you breathe.

Or, by becoming aware of the breath
through the slight sensation it creates
when entering or exiting your nostrils

(either way your eyes should still be
closed and focused at the point between
the eyebrows - the spiritual eye.)

Don't attempt to control the breath
in any way. Simply observe it and
be aware of it.

Take notice, that as you observe
the breath, the breath begins to slow
down and then becomes longer.

As it does, you naturally begin
to relax. The slower the breath
the deeper the relaxation,
the slower the breath
your mind too - begins
to relax more deeply.

*As your body and mind begin
to relax, your thoughts also begin
to still/relax.*

*Only when your mind becomes deeply
Relaxed and your thoughts become still,
begin to:*

**visualize yourself living fully
and completely in your optimum
potential - the life of your deepest
dreams and highest inspirations.**

*Whatever your focus and priority be at this time,
in life, whether it be: success, abundance,
expansion, excellence, joy, and/or a fulfilling
relationship, a loving family, a thriving business
or career and/or simply a life of happiness
and harmony.*

**The true success to your visualization is not
only based upon your ability - to envision
(visualize) that reality but most
importantly to FEEL it - NOW!**

*Visualize how it would feel to be in the complete
accomplishment/joy of this experience. Drink in
and bathe in that feeling until nothing else
exists but the complete **UP** feeling and inner
satisfaction of that accomplishment...*

**allow yourself to bask in the fulfillment
of that accomplishment & joy for as long
as possible.**

Stay there as long as you can remain relaxed,
uplifted, and in joy, 1 min., 5 min., 20 min.

Then slowly, to bring the visualization
to completion - again do
the 1 - 8 count breath cycle:
inhale 1 - 8 count
hold the breathe 1 - 8 count
and exhale 1 - 8 count several times.

Sit another minute or two
absorbed in that uplifting feeling
of complete wonder, achievement, and joy.

Do this as often as you like, the more the better.
The more, the faster you will bring your
inspiration and dreams towards manifestation.

*"To carry on a successful business
one must have imagination.
He must see things in a vision,
a dream of the whole thing."*

~ Charles M. Schwab

10

To Achieve the Best Results
with Visualization...
and Beyond

To accomplish great things
we must first dream,
then visualize
the life that you most want.

See it, feel it, believe in it...then act.
Make your mental blue print,
and then begin to build.

1

To achieve the best results with visualization it
is best to enter into the visualization experience
by clearing all distracting thoughts and
preoccupations.

This makes the visualizations all the more
powerful: when our thoughts are still and we can
focus with strong intention, inner clarity, and deep
relaxation.

That is the importance of allowing yourself the
necessary time to quiet the mind, and to focus
your attention through the 1- 8 breathing exercise
count while observing the breath.

2

Ideally you want to enter into the experience of creative visualization with **complete openness** - and the true awareness that all life is full with **infinite possibilities** and that *ALL* **things are possible**.

3

So to begin, always get to the highest, clearest, most relaxed state of being you possibly can. Then put your full attention, focus, and concentration into creating that all powerful visualization will begin to that bring your new reality into manifestation.

~ O ~

As mentioned above there are many types of creative visualizations, for the purposes of this book I have shared one of the most powerful manifesting visualizations available - to give you a direct experience of the energy and power both of visualization and manifesting.

By practicing and applying visualizations - you will find they will each have their own unique power and effectiveness.

Choose or create a visualization that will most directly begin to manifest your new reality, whether that may be in this moment - success, prosperity, abundance, relationships, or inner peace, etc.

Of course, along with both affirmations and visualizations, one must also take action.

One must always be on the look out for, or create, *ANY* potential opportunity to enrich one's life and further one's inspired goals.

However, the deepest and most powerful way of taking action has already been invoked and begun, on the energetic level - by planting the seeds of positive, powerful, and effective, affirmations & visualizations, and allowing them to grow with formidable clear focus, and with strong conscious intention.

And by feeling and believing as though YOUR goals and dreams have already become a thriving, living reality.

Thus creating an concise blueprint of attainment that brings them into visible fruition.

As Michael Dooley shares in his insightful book:
Infinite Possibilities:
The Art of Living your Dreams:

" *Visualization powerfully impacts your thought process and ultimately your belief system.*

Whatever it is you want today,
to the degree that it is possible
and feasible - act as if it's already in your life."

This thread of thought "act as if it's already in your life" is wholly significant and echoed again and again... because it is an essential core component that begins to bring into your life the actualization and manifestation of your highest inspirations and deepest dreams!

"We always attract into our lives whatever we think about most, believe in most strongly, expect on the deepest level, and imagine most vividly."

~ Shakti Gawain

"All the breaks you need in life wait within your imagination,

Imagination is the workshop of your mind, capable of turning mind energy into accomplishment and wealth. "

~ Napoleon Hill

11

The True Value of Meditation!

*"Meditation opens the mind,
to the greatest of life's mysteries,
it opens the heart to embrace
the power of harmony
within all life."*

When practiced regularly, meditation will be one
of your most powerful allies, to create the life you
aspire to! It helps us to both focus and
concentrate - and strengthens these *absolutely
necessary - to - succeed* qualities.

**Meditation is the most effective way
to enter into and access an awareness of
inner clarity.**

Again, inner clarity *is* the first requisite and
essential component in generating and creating
the life of your dreams. Inner clarity is often the
main omission that keeps us from bringing our
plans, efforts and goals into manifestation.

Along with inner clarity, the many benefits
of meditation include an ever-increasing sense
of inner calmness, radiant well-being, expanded
awareness, and deep relaxation.

The first tell tale sign of experiencing a *successful*

meditation is a sense of radiant peace, and/or a feeling of deep inner calm.

A deep inner calm and a sense of radiant peace that allow YOU to relax fully and deeply - on all levels!

As we fill our days with continual busyness, along with all the daily demands placed upon us - when do we really make/find the time to relax deeply and **fully** enjoy the wonder and beauty of life?

Meditation allows **deep relaxation** into our lives. And as you relax and go deeper within you will discover –

true meditation puts YOU in touch, and in harmony with the very source of inspiration itself. True meditation reveals levels of clarity and possibility you may not have yet experienced, or perhaps were previously inaccessible to you.

Remember that inspiration is not only one of the principal components for creating success and happiness in your life, it is the primary spark that ignites all the other components –

imagination, creativity, and passion, and gives birth to manifesting the life of our dreams.

This then, is the True Value of Meditation!

So, lets give it a try, that you may begin to experience its effectiveness and benefits right away.

Meditation Exercise:

The beginning of this exercise is almost exactly the same as the visualization exercise 1, so if you've made time to practice the visualization technique this one will come easily...

*find a place to sit quietly
and comfortably, either in a chair, or on a pillow,
whichever is most pleasing to you.*

*Make sure your spine is straight
and your body is relaxed...*

*and as with the visualization exercise:
close your eyes focusing your mentally gaze
at the spiritual eye - the point between
the eyebrows.*

*Inhale, counting mentally from 1 - 8
hold the breathe, counting mentally from 1 - 8
and exhale as you count mentally 1 - 8.*

*Do this cycle of inhaling, holding,
and releasing the breath 3 - 4 times.
Continue to breath naturally
and mentally observe the
natural flow of your breath.*

*You may become aware of the flow
of your breath through mental observation*

of the rise and fall of your belly
as you breathe.

Or, by becoming aware of the breath
through the slight sensation it creates
when entering or exiting your nostrils

(either way your eyes should still be
closed and focused at the point between the
eyebrows - the spiritual eye.)

Don't attempt to control the breath in any way.
Simply observe it and be aware of it.

Take notice that as you observe the
breath, the breath begins to slow down
and then becomes longer.

As it does,
you naturally begin to relax.
The slower the breath
the deeper the relaxation.
As your breath slows,
your mind too begins to relax
more deeply.

As your body and mind begin to relax,
your thoughts also begin to still/relax.

Only when your mind becomes deeply
Relaxed and your thoughts become still,
begin the actual meditation technique
offered below.

**This is where the meditation exercise
differs from the visualization technique.**

*On the next inhalation, mentally affirm
the word " still "*

*on the next exhalation, mentally affirm
the word " ness."*

*Continue to repeat " still "
with each new incoming breath*

*and " ness " with each release
of the breath.*

*If unexpected noises or disturbances
of any kind interrupt or distract you,
just calmly, patiently, bring your attention
back into the present moment*

*and begin repeating "still"...
with your next inhalation and "ness"
with your next exhalation.*

*If thoughts of the past or future
interrupt or disturb your mind -
again, calmly, patiently,*

*bring your attention back,
into the present moment -
and begin repeating "still"...
with your next inhalation
and "ness" with your next exhalation.*

Try to do this for 5 -10 minutes, longer, if possible.

Try to do this at least until you feel that first sweet glimmer of "radiant peace, and/or inner calm," and then allow yourself to stay in that inspired state of mind for as long as possible – *see below.*

To end the meditation, remain in the experience of radiant peace and inner calm for as long as possible.

Then do the 1-8 count inhale, hold the breath, and exhale breathing exercises for 3 rounds.

This helps to bridge our awareness from the inner world into the outer world.

Then open your eyes when ready...and as you get up and begin your daily activities retain that inner quietude for as long as possible.

Meditate 5 - 10 minutes to start with and gradually increase the time.

Remember: the longer you can remain in meditation and feel the radiant peace and inner stillness, the more you will feel the serene and tranquil qualities of radiant peace and inner calmness throughout the day.

They don't just stop, when "meditation time" is over. The more meditation becomes a part of your life, the more YOUR inner clarity will increase exponentially.

Through meditation these qualities: *radiant well-being, expanded awareness, inner calmness* and deep relaxation all become absorbed and integrated into your every day, moment by moment, life experience.

With the end results being enhanced inner clarity, dynamic optimum potential, & true happiness.

Listed below are other qualities you can choose to focus on during meditation. Simply replace the word " still - ness " with one of these qualities during meditation... to further develop and absorb these attributes into your life,

But only after you feel that you have gained a sense for, and a depth of experience with the still - ness meditation, first!

Calm - ness
Open - ness
Happi - ness
Sweet - ness
Tender - ness
Loveli -ness
Hopeful - ness
Joyful - ness.

12

To Achieve
the Finest Meditation Results

"Inner silence promotes clarity of mind;
it makes us value the inner world;
It trains us to go inside to the source
of peace and inspiration when we
are faced with problems and challenges."

~ Deepak Chopra

To experience the best meditation results:

1

**Meditation is best and most easily experienced
within one hour of the transitional times
of day.**

This includes morning at 6 am, 12 noon, 6 pm,
and 12 midnight. This has to do with the earths
electro - magnetic field. At these times of day the
earth's electro magnetics are not as strong as the
rest of the day, they weaken while in transition
from one part of the day to the next.

When their influence is lessened it is easier to
meditate because their effect has less direct
impact upon you.

2

Create a "Quiet or Sacred Space" to meditate in your home.

Creating a "quiet or sacred space" in your home makes it easier to meditate especially if it is the only activity done in that location. Remember, our thoughts are vibrations and we draw similar vibrations to us.

By creating a place of uplifting and inspiring thoughts - these qualities naturally becomes the feeling and the experience whenever we are in or revisit that space, therefore making it is easier to meditate.

Most people make a quiet space in the their bedroom. This can easily be done by partitioning off a section of the room with portable shoji screens, hanging curtains, a beautiful cloth, or something similar.

3

Cover the chair or pillow that you are sitting upon to meditate with wool, or silk. A wool blanket or a silk shawl works great!

Wool and silk help protect you from the earth's magnetic field and allow you to meditate more easily and fruitfully.

4

Best to allow two to three hours after eating, before meditating in earnest.

Otherwise, your digestive tract will be in high competition with your ability to meditate successfully.

5

Allow yourself to sit in the "radiant peace and/or inner clam" of meditation, for as long as possible.

Allow yourself to retain that inner experience for as long as the **" UP"** feeling inspires you. In doing so, all the benefits of meditation: inner clarity, an ever-increasing sense of radiant well-being, expanded awareness/ perception, and deep relaxation, *become absorbed into, and become a part* of your everyday life.

Otherwise, it's like eating a big wonderful meal and then immediately getting up and going jogging. It simply takes away from the richness and depth of the overall experience.

Meditation brings wisdom –
lack of meditation leaves ignorance.
Know well what leads you forward
and what holds you back,
and choose the path that leads to wisdom.

~ Buddha

13

The Importance of Intuition

*"Your inner knowing
is your only true compass!"*

**Intuition is of the highest quality
of awareness - where " inner clarity "
and "inner knowing" reside,**

**as well as the place of true perception -
where the portal of unlimited potential
opens and reveals that
ALL THINGS ARE POSSIBLE!**

Being in an intuitive state of awareness,
is to experience a level of consciousness that
allows us to be continually connected to the
source of **ALL** inspiration.

Through Intuition - insights and inspiration reveal
themselves most clearly and guide us forward
each step of the way.

*It is from inner stillness that intuition grows,
and blossoms.*

The more we develop our "intuitive awareness" the
more we begin to feel and experience a very clear
sense of inner guidance, as well as a very real
sense of the "unity of all life" - a feeling of true

harmony in the world around us.

Born of the inner harmony emerging within
us - through our newly acquired techniques
of affirmations, visualizations, and meditation.

**Once developed, intuitive awareness can be
applied towards any endeavor.**

If we take the time to explore and develop the art
of intuition, if we take the time to understand
and establish this extraordinary way of
approaching life, we will find from the onset
that we clearly have the advantage in manifesting
a creative, inspired, successful, and joyful life.

*"Your time is limited,
so don't waste it
living someone else's life.*

*Don't be trapped by dogma -
which is living with the results
of other people's thinking.*

*Don't let the noise of others' opinions
drown out your own inner voice.*

*And most important,
have the courage to follow
your heart and intuition."*

~ Steve Jobs

14

Exercise to Develop Intuition

*"The intuitive mind is a sacred gift
and the rational mind is a faithful servant.
We have created a society that honors the
servant and has forgotten the gift."*

~ Albert Einstein

**Surprise! If you've spent time practicing the
meditation technique, the exercise to develop
intuition will come easy. It's the same exercise
as the meditation exercise, with a different but
very powerful emphasis.**

*Simply begin by sitting
in a comfortable position.*

*Either in a chair, or on a pillow,
whichever is most pleasing to you.*

*Make sure your spine is straight
and your body is relaxed...*

*close your eyes and take a few
deep breathes.*

*Continue as like the meditation exercise
with eyes closed, placing your mental gaze*

gently upward at the point between the eyebrows.

Inhale, counting mentally from 1 - 8
hold the breathe, counting mentally from 1 - 8
and exhale as you count mentally 1 - 8.

Do this cycle of inhaling, holding,
and releasing the breath 3 - 4 times
then mentally observe
the natural flow of your breath.

You may become aware of the flow
of your breath through mental observation
of the rise and fall of your belly as you breathe.

Or, by becoming aware of the breath
through the slight sensation it creates
when entering or exiting your nostrils.

Either way your eyes should still be closed
and focused at the point between the eyebrows.

Don't attempt to control the breath in any way.
Simply observe it and be aware of it.
Take notice that as you observe the breath,
the breath begins to slow down
and then becomes longer.

As it does, you naturally begin to relax.
The slower the breath
the deeper the relaxation,
the slower the breath,
your mind too begins
to relax more deeply.

As your body and mind begin to relax,
your thoughts also begin to still/relax.

Only when your mind becomes deeply relaxed
and your thoughts become still, begin the actual
meditation technique offered below:

on the next inhalation, mentally affirm
the word " still "

on the next exhalation, mentally affirm
the word " ness."

Continue to repeat " still " with each
new incoming breath

and " ness " with each release
of the breath.

Unexpected noises or disturbances
of any kind may interrupt or distract you.

If so, just calmly, patiently, bring your attention
back into the present moment... begin repeating
"still" with your next inhalation and "ness" with
your next exhalation.

If thoughts of the past or future interrupt or disturb
your mind, again, calmly, patiently, bring your
attention back into the moment...

begin repeating "still" with your next inhalation
and "ness" with your next exhalation.

**This is where the intuition exercise
differs from the meditation technique.**

*As you get more and more into the flow
and rhythm of the "still - ness" meditation
exercise, you will notice, as the body relaxes
and the mind becomes still - the breath
slows down.*

*The inhalation and exhalation of the breath
gets longer and the PAUSE between each
breath also gets longer.*

*Become completely aware of this PAUSE
between the breath.*

*The PAUSE... between the inhalation and the
exhalation.*

*As the PAUSE... between the inhalation and
exhalation become longer, relax into Pause
for as long as possible.*

*As you go deeper still, the PAUSE... between
each breath continues to become longer.*

*Allow yourself to stay in the relaxation of this
PAUSE... between each breath, naturally,
without strain or effort.*

*It is in this open, deepened, relaxed, and very
"still" state of awareness, between the
inhalation and the exhalation
of each breath... that intuition is born.*

The more you allow yourself time to " be present "
in this place between the breath in deep
relaxation, the more rapidly intuition is developed.

Intuition then becomes a part of your everyday,
ever - more increasingly inspired life.

It is best to do this exercise - the meditation
technique and the intuition exercise together
for 10 - 20 minutes - to begin with.

Longer, as you become more familiar
with the practice and it naturally becomes
a part and flow of your daily activities.

*To end the meditation, remain in the radiant peace
and inner calm for as long as possible.*

*Then do the 1-8 count, inhale, hold the breathe,
exhale, breathing exercises for 3 rounds.*

*Then open your eyes when ready...
and as you get up and begin your daily activities
retain that inner quietude for as long as possible.*

All the - *To Achieve the Finest Meditation Results*
points to remember - as described in Chapter 13 of
this book, apply to the intuition exercise as well.

To Recap:

1. True meditation does not begin until the mind
and emotions are stilled.

2. Once stilled - we can begin to experience a deepening sense of inner calmness and radiant peace.

3. In meditation, the mind and heart experience an expanded sense of well being, openness/ receptivity.

4. In inner stillness, ever - new creativity, deep inspiration, and intuition are born!

*"The heart knows what it wants,
and it often makes no sense.
Intuition, creativity, and listening are
all imperative in creating an inspired life."*

~ Jonathan H. Ellerby

15

Points to Remember!

*"We cannot solve our problems
with the same thinking
we used when we created them."*

~ Albert Einstein

1

To initiate real change in your life - simply start
the process by enthusiastically embracing *new*
thoughts of the *new* life you want to create, as well
as initiating new choices that will take you in the
direction you want your life to go.

To help focus new thoughts, boldly repeat
affirmations with sincere intention and deep
concentration. As you begin to strongly avow
your affirmations, you are **NOW** creating *NEW*
thought patterns... that form the creation of your
new life.

That take the place of the old thought patterns
that have kept you from creating the life you
desire, a life of fulfillment, success, and
abundance!

2

To help magnetize the events, people, and
conditions that will help you create the life you

aspire to: **visualize**, not so much the exact details of what you want but rather the feeling and energy - **of having it in your life already... of the complete joy of that accomplishment.**

Allow yourself to **FEEL** that experience as if it is, in truth, **already a living, breathing and thriving reality... NOW!**

3

Meditation is one of your best and most powerful allies. Meditation helps to develop inner clarity, a sense of radiant well - being, expanded awareness and deep relaxation.

Meditation is also the foundation for cultivating, generating, and strengthening intuition.

As you go deeper within, you will discover – that true meditation reveals ever - increasing levels of clarity and optimum potential you may not yet have experienced or perhaps, were previously inaccessible to you.

True meditation puts us in touch, and in harmony, with the very source of inspiration and creativity itself.

4

Intuition is of the highest quality of awareness - where "inner clarity" and "intuitive awareness" reside, as well as the place of true

**perception - where the portal of infinite
possibility opens and reveals that
ALL THINGS ARE POSSIBLE!**

*"Our intuition is creative
and flourishing,
if we but know how to use it,
intuition connects us
to a richer world,
a world full of enchantment
and a sense of the miraculous."*

16

Giving Yourself
Quality Permission(s)

*"Always leave enough time in your life
to do something that makes you happy,
satisfied, even joyous.
That has more of an effect on well-being
than any other single factor. "*

~ Paul Hawken

We all live such busy lives... we all get lost at
times, in our day to day demands and needs.
As you enthusiastically and energetically go forth
with thoughts of creating abundance and focusing
on your dreams and inspirations be sure to take
the time to allow yourself a few
quality permissions.

Quality permissions will allow more enjoyment in
your life, and will enhance and nurture your over -
all intent, to create the life of your dreams.

1

Permissions that allow you:
to do the things that inspire you the most.

2

Permissions that allow you:
to feel nourished and uplifted.

3

Permissions that allow you:
**to feel a part of the unique role you play
in the universe.**

4

Permissions that allow you:
**an uninterrupted sense of inner balance
and alignment.**

5

Permissions that allow you:
**to LAUGH a lot...to have FUN, and to fully
enjoy the beauty and wonder of life.**

Whether, spending time with friends that
encourage us, support us, and nurture us,
or taking a walk in the beauty and magnificence
of nature.

Whether spending the day absorbed in silent
contemplation, or reading an uplifting book, or
enjoying an inspiring movie, or listening to music
that uplifts the spirit.

6

Permissions that allow you:
**to open your heart and to learn to love
courageously.**

By expanding our love, our heart serves as both
a transmitter and a magnet. As a transmitter (with
all our new perspectives, techniques, and
exercises) we are sending out unending positive
thoughts and vibrations into the world.

As a magnet, we draw to ourselves all the right
people, circumstances, and conditions
**that will move us exponential forward in the
best way possible.**

7

Give **YOURSELF** permissions that allow you:
**To do those things that constantly - remind
you - and allow you to move forward into your
highest aspirations, and deepest dreams.**

That remind you - that a life of inspiration, joy,
and abundance **is not only possible, but within
your reach.**

In doing so, your optimum energy potential **and
true happiness will be activated and achieved**
as a natural outpouring of your whole - hearted
efforts and dedicated intentions.

Obviously, the above permissions are all geared
toward the individual where all real/true change

begins.

However, consider and imagine if everyone in your work place were "uplifted" - and living and working with the inspiration, intention, and techniques shared in this book!

A natural flow of **energetic synthesis:** inspiration, balance, and harmony - equaling optimum potential would be created among individuals in the work place.

It would indeed be a whole new and wonderful world, both for the individuals and the overall excellence and success of the business/ organization.

Creating Quality Permission(s) for Business & Organizations

How do you creative and develop new business/organization permissions that foster and facilitate inspiration and help grow your business towards and into productivity, profitability, and ever greater success?

Permissions with an openness to create the best possible business/organization - like anything else successful - this will take focus, quality & energy.

The success and well - being of your business/organization depend on it, as the rewards - are an inspired energy flow, with a fresh creative approach - that allows for a successful and a thriving enterprise!

**Ideas for allowing
and/or creating quality permissions
for your business/organization:**

Create the circumstances that will allow for both a strong shared group focus and inspired ideas to naturally flow.

Here are a few ideas towards facilitating this:

A company/organization picnic

A company/organization " fun " party

A no - holds - bar brainstorming party

A company/organization " retreat "

A company/organization " spa " experience

Ideally, the company/organization could/would
provide for the well - being of the employees -
allowing some, if not all, of these experiences to
take place on company time.

In other words, during working hours
in which the participants would be paid
as like, normal working hours.

To make these events meaningful, beneficial, and
"real," the business or organization **needs create
new permissions** that will work specifically and
inspirationally for **your** business or organization.

In doing so, you will be taking the first steps
towards creating and manifesting
a working environment that has the potential
to become so energetic, dynamic, and magnetic,
that its working vitality, increased productivity,
and end result - can only draw great success,
abundance, and fulfillment.

**Coming together is a beginning.
Keeping together is progress.
Working together is success.**

18

Guidelines for Developing a Successful Company/ Business/Organization

1. Develop an inspiring vision:
Excellent companies/organizations
make a serious effort to shape values.

The right values clearly expressed
help define the organization,
and its direction(s).

These values become clear to everyone involved
with the company/organization,
as well as each of your clients/customers.

2. Foster cooperation, harmony, & respect
in the dynamic workplace/environment...
building an effective team.

Cooperation and respect will create
the primary source of productivity gains.

3. Being loyalty to one another -
an extension of the number 2 guideline,
and an extension of yourself.

4. Work (cooperatively) towards
the achievement of lasting results.

5. Combine inspiration and intuition
with common sense.

6.Find creative solutions to difficult problems.

7. Run ahead of the pack with vision
& experimentation:

A successful company needs
to be efficient at the basics
and innovative on a regular basis.

Enterprise is first creativity.
You need creativity to see what's out there
and shape it to your advantage.
You need creativity to look
at the world a little differently.
You need creativity to take
a different approach,
to be different.

~ Jim Rohn

The heart and soul of the company
is creativity and innovation.

~ Robert Iger

19

Ahhh, So Many Blessings!

"From a place of stillness, rises potential.
From the place of potential,
emerges possibility.
Where there is possibility,
there are unceasing choices:
courses of action, options,
opportunities, and prospects."

Imagine your world
orchestrated in such a way
as to receive unending
help and support
for your business/organization.

Imagine, every obstacle
an opportunity,

every challenge an occasion
for taking one big step

closer to the fulfillment
of your dreams and goals.

Imagine every person
a friend rather than
a stranger or a threat

and the world then begins
to emerge a place of increasing
wonder and beauty.

This new way of perceiving and flourishing in the
world has emerged through a simple shift of intent
and perspective: *inspired, dreamed, shaped, and
brought* into being by you.

You who are courageous enough to effect, initiate,
and create the desired changes that give life/
business/organization and make your
dreams come true.

You who are steadfast enough
to make the transition
that would shift your life towards and into,
excellence and peak optimum potential.

**In doing so, you not only make your world
a far better place, but prevail in making *the*
whole world a better place.**

*By bringing into the world your vision - through your
dedicated efforts; by bringing into the world your
new reality - manifested by your new choices;
by bringing into the world the positive impacts and
dynamic energy that gave life to your dreams - you
have altered, rearranged, and transformed
your life by unquestionably listening to your highest
inspiration(s) and pursuing your deepest dreams.*

And in doing so,
YOU have become an inspiration,
by touching the hearts and lives of others in ways

that show they too, *can* live the life of **their** inspiration and create the life of **their** dreams.

This is the time for CELEBRATION –
for honoring your true Self,
for listening to your dreams.
for honoring all your efforts

This is the time for CONGRATULATIONS !

As you continue forth on your wondrous journey, always remember - in the pursuit of living your dreams being in optimum potential, and living your highest inspirations,

there are fewer things more powerful –
than intention followed by action.

*That every time you make a focused affirmation; each time you visualize and feel the complete and unutterable joy **of a new living, thriving reality,***

*every time you are positive and **your energy is UP,** you open **yourself UP** to draw upon and align yourself with the very <u>source</u> of inspiration.*

*You open **yourself UP** to draw upon your imagination, passion, creativity, & inner clarity: the energetics of optimum potential.*

Allowing yourself to dive deep into the sea of unlimited possibility - that is constantly there for you - to draw upon at every turn.

That awaits you: to take the first whole - hearted

step in creating the life of your dreams... that will help give your life new direction each step of the way, as well as support and encourage you to live in the fullness of your optimal potential and achieve a life of true happiness!

WHAT ARE YOU WAITING FOR?

Ignite the **creative** spark of **bold** intention, and see how your life/business/organization begins to change and unfold. Like the proverbial caterpillar, transformed from the depths of the unknown - into the magnificent beauty of the butterfly,

CELEBRATE as your new life emerges, blooms, flourishes, and thrives filled with accomplishment and success - into the life /business/organization of your greatest inspiration and deepest dreams!

Ahhh, what a blessing indeed!

Excellence is...
Caring more than others
think is wise.

Risking more than others
think is safe.

Dreaming more than others
think is practical.

Expecting more than others
think is possible.

"As we look ahead into the next century,
leaders will be those who empower others".

~ Bill Gates

"Only those who attempt the absurd
will achieve the impossible."

~ M.C Escher

About the Author
Robert Frutos

Robert has owned a number of dynamic
and successful businesses:
a Gardening/Landscaping Company,
Handyman Service, Reforestation Business,
Plumbing Enterprise, Construction and
Remodeling Operation
& Heart of Nature Greeting Cards

Robert is currently a nature photographer
and is the owner of the longest running Photo
Tour businessin the state of Hawaii -
Heart of Nature Photography & Photo Tours

He is also the author of numerous books
(see page 3) on many subjects including
**"Photographing Nature in Hawaii:
Capturing the Beauty and Spirit of the Islands"**
Published by Island Heritage Publishing.

Robert teaches photography related subjects,
As well as classes and workshops that focus
on Self - enrichment & Self – empowerment,

to share inspiration and techniques with anyone interested in building their best life possible.

Through classes, workshops, cd's, and books, Robert aspires to help make your inspiration, hopes, and dreams a reality.

Robert's passion, inspiration, and sharing with others - the keys that make for a happy and successful life - has found vast unending fulfillment.

Robert resides on the big island of Hawaii where he is currently and fully - living the life of his dreams!

Don't wait until tomorrow
to scale the mountain of your dreams.

DO IT NOW!

~ J. Donald Walters

Made in the USA
Monee, IL
19 March 2025

14251497R00066